Stress Management

Strategies for Emotional Fitness

Third Edition

Merrill F. Raber, MSW, Ph.D.
and George Dyck, M.D.
with Barbara Preheim, MSW

A Crisp Fifty-Minute™ Series Book

This Fifty-Minute™ Book is designed to be "read with a pencil." It is an excellent workbook for self-study as well as classroom learning. All material is copyright-protected and cannot be duplicated without permission from the publisher.
Therefore, be sure to order a copy for every training participant by contacting:

THOMSON
★
™
NETg

1-800-442-7477 ◆ 25 Thomson Place, Boston, MA ◆ www.courseilt.com

Stress Management

Strategies for Emotional Fitness

Third Edition

Merrill F. Raber, MSW, Ph.D.
and George Dyck, M.D.
with Barbara Preheim, MSW

CREDITS:

Senior Editor:	**Debbie Woodbury**
Editor:	**Ann Gosch**
Assistant Editor:	**Genevieve McDermott**
Production Manager:	**Stephanie Porreca**
Design:	**Nicole Phillips**
Production Artist:	**Rich Lehl**

For more information contact:

NETg
25 Thomson Place
Boston, MA 02210

Or find us on the Web at **www.courseilt.com**

For permission to use material from this text or product, submit a request online at: www.thomsonrights.com

Any additional questions about permissions can be submitted by e-mail to: thomsonrights@thomson.com

Trademarks

Crisp Fifty-Minute Series is a trademark of NETg.

Some of the product names and company names used in this book have been used for identification purposes only and may be trademarks or registered trademarks of their respective manufacturers and sellers.

Disclaimer

NETg reserves the right to revise this publication and make changes from time to time in its content without notice.

ISBN 1-4188-4710-0
Library of Congress Catalog Card Number 2005922986
Printed in the United States of America
2 3 4 5 08 07 06

Learning Objectives for

STRESS MANAGEMENT

The objectives for *Stress Management* are listed below. They have been developed to guide the user to the core issues covered in this book.

The objectives of this book are to help the user:

1) Define stress and understand its effects on emotional health

2) Examine strategies for coping with stress

3) Employ mindfulness meditation techniques

4) Make personal contacts positive and meaningful

5) Explore ways to attain and maintain emotional maturity

Assessing Progress

NETg has developed a Crisp Series **assessment** that covers the fundamental information presented in this book. A 25-item, multiple-choice and true/false questionnaire allows the reader to evaluate his or her comprehension of the subject matter.

To buy the assessment and answer key, go to www.courseilt.com and search on the book title or via the assessment format, or call 1-800-442-7477.

Assessments should not be used in any employee-selection process.

About the Authors

Merrill F. Raber, MSW, Ph.D., is recently retired after 40 years in the field of mental health, organization development, and mediation. In addition to private practice he had also been associated with Prairie View Community Mental Health Center, Newton, Kansas, and was Clinical Associate Professor, Family and Community Medicine, Kansas University School of Medicine-Wichita.

George Dyck, M.D., is a psychiatrist in private practice. He is a former medical director of Prairie View Community Mental Health Center, Newton, Kansas. He is also professor emeritus, Psychiatry and Behavioral Sciences, Kansas University School of Medicine-Wichita.

Barbara Preheim, MSW, is a clinical social worker in practice with the Bert Nash Mental Health Center, Lawrence, Kansas.

Preface

During the past decade considerable attention has been devoted to the importance of good physical health. The results have been impressive. Large numbers of people now exercise regularly, watch their diets, and take other preventative health measures.

This book was developed to focus similar attention on managing stress to maintain good emotional health. Many of the principles presented in this book can be developed and practiced like a thoughtful exercise program or diet.

The pressures of life are many. It is important to remember that everyone experiences some stress. Stress is normal and, properly managed, can be useful. This book will focus on finding the level of stress that may be useful for you and teaching you ways to recognize and avoid stress beyond that level. Other topics will help you understand the basic ingredients of emotional health, improve self-awareness and self-image, and clarify the link between physical wellness and emotional wellness.

One reading will simply point you in the right direction. Completing the various exercises and activities can be a significant step toward self-awareness and growth in the challenging arena of your emotional health.

Good luck!

Merrill F. Raber, MSW, Ph.D.
George Dyck, M.D.
Barbara Preheim, MSW

Table of Contents

P A R T 1

Understanding Stress

The Effects of Stress on Emotional Health

Stress is a part of life. Life today is complex and it is impossible to avoid stress. How much stress individuals encounter and how they deal with it has a direct connection with emotional health. This part will look at stress and its many dimensions.

Stress is what we experience internally in response to a situation we find hard to deal with. Most of us handle routine stress readily. In other words, we are able to "handle the situation." We can resolve our feelings and dissipate the tension.

Stress is essentially *within* us even though we may perceive it as coming from outside. This is why not everyone experiences the same circumstances as stressful. What is stressful for one person may not be for another. In this sense, it may be counterproductive to tell someone not to worry about a situation if you do not consider the same situation as stressful. We all react to situations differently; it is part of being human.

Stress Management and Emotional Fitness

Stress is a learning laboratory that constantly teaches us about how to handle the difficulties we encounter. In the same way that exercising keeps our bodies physically fit, dealing effectively with the demands that affect our emotions keeps us emotionally fit.

Anxiety is a signal that we are under stress. If this feeling keeps recurring, stress is not being dealt with effectively. For example, if you find yourself continually upset and angry, it would be worthwhile to determine the source of your anger and then find an appropriate way to deal with it. Otherwise your feelings will build and produce negative effects.

When our feelings build beyond a certain point, we begin to experience strain. If the situation we find troublesome disappears, the feeling of stress goes away. If the pressure does not let up, however, we eventually will show signs of emotional and physical exhaustion.

Expected life events that we all encounter are often stressful. These events include the entire range of experiences: a new birth, entering school, marriage, divorce, and the loss of a family member.

Sudden, unexpected catastrophic events are well-known causes of stress. Situations that result in our chronically feeling bad, either about ourselves or others, also can result in stress.

Expressing emotions is often difficult. The ability to recognize stress and then learn to manage it through an appropriate expression of emotions is extremely important in coping with stress.

People who continually hold their emotions inside often "boil over" at inappropriate times. This may damage their relationships with others. This seems to occur most often where stress has built up over a period of time. One way to help avoid this is to talk things over before the "boiling point" is reached.

Recognizing Stress

Different people recognize stress in different ways. For some, stress is a set of feelings that makes them aware that "something is not right." For others, stress comes from a series of stressful events. For still others, stress might be more accurately identified as a lifestyle, or lifestyle choice, that affects themselves and others. Finally, some people see stress as the resulting physical symptoms. Recognizing that all of these describe the same process is helpful in understanding stress.

Ways to identify stress include the following:

Feelings	**Lifestyle**
Restlessness	Intensive drive
Keyed-up feeling	Aggressiveness
Anxiety	Impatience
Depression	Workaholism
Crisis Events	**Physical Symptoms**
Death of a family member	Headaches
Separation	Fatigue
Divorce	Insomnia
Business failure	Hypertension
	Abdominal discomfort
	Excessive eating or loss of appetite

Testing Your Stress Level

Our lives are filled with both happy and sad events. Many of us do not realize, however, that all of life's changes can result in stress on both our physical and emotional health.

Changes occur in everyone's life. Some are everyday experiences. Others are not-so-common. All can cause stress and anxiety.

The list that follows is a stress test that was developed by Drs. Thomas H. Holmes and Richard H. Rahe to help people understand what causes stress in their lives. Place a check (✓) beside each event that you have experienced in the last year and then add the attached point values.

HOLMES-RAHE STRESS TEST*			
Rank	Event	Value	Your Score
1.	Death of spouse	100	_____
2.	Divorce	73	_____
3.	Marital separation	65	_____
4.	Jail term	63	_____
5.	Death of close family member	63	_____
6.	Personal injury or illness	53	_____
7.	Marriage	50	_____
8.	Fired from work	47	_____
9.	Marital reconciliation	45	_____
10.	Retirement	45	_____
11.	Change in family member's health	44	_____
12.	Pregnancy	40	_____
13.	Sex difficulties	39	_____
14.	Addition to family	39	_____
15.	Business readjustment	39	_____
16.	Change in financial status	38	_____
17.	Death of close friend	37	_____
18.	Change in number of marital arguments	35	_____
19.	Mortgage or loan over $10,000	31	_____
20.	Foreclosure of mortgage or loan	30	_____
21.	Change in work responsibilities	29	_____
22.	Son or daughter leaving home	29	_____
23.	Trouble with in-laws	29	_____
24.	Outstanding personal achievement	28	_____
25.	Spouse begins or stops work	26	_____

Rank	Event	Value	Your Score
26.	Starting or finishing school	26	_____
27.	Change in living conditions	25	_____
28.	Revision of personal habits	24	_____
29.	Trouble with boss	23	_____
30.	Change in work hours, conditions	20	_____
31.	Change in residence	20	_____
32.	Change in schools	20	_____
33.	Change recreational habits	19	_____
34.	Change in church activities	19	_____
35.	Change in social activities	18	_____
36.	Mortgage or loan under $10,000	18	_____
37.	Change in sleeping habits	16	_____
38.	Change in number of family gatherings	15	_____
39.	Change in eating habits	14	_____
40.	Vacation	13	_____
41.	Christmas season	12	_____
42.	Minor violation of the law	11	_____
		Total	_____

SCORING: Add up the point values of all the items checked. If your score is 300 or more, you stand an almost 80% chance of getting sick in the near future as a result of the events. If your score is 150 to 299, the chances are about 50%. If less than 150, the chances are about 30%.

This scale suggests that life changes require an effort to adapt and then to regain stability. This process probably saps energy the body would ordinarily use to maintain itself, so susceptibility to illness increases.

Thomas H. Holmes and Richard R. Rahe, "Social Readjustment Rating Scale," *Journal of Psychosomatic Research II,* (1967): 214. Reprinted with permission.

Identifying Behavior Patterns

Considerable research has been focused on two distinct personality types, Type A and Type B, over the past several decades. You can recognize Type A as people who are generally more competitive, restless, and quick to anger. Their counterparts, Type B, show behaviors that are calmer and less rushed by the day's events.

Type A behavior has been described by researchers and cardiologists Meyer Friedman, M.D., and Ray H. Rosenman, M.D., as the kind of stressful lifestyle that is much more likely to lead to heart disease. On the other hand, recent research suggests Type A individuals may be better prepared to survive a heart attack when it does occur.

Type B behavior seems to produce fewer physical problems related to stress. Type Bs tend to be less pressured and often deal with others more easily, yet they rise to the "top" as frequently as do Type As. They also seem to enjoy the little things in life that add meaning.

We know that it is possible to modify our behavior and make a significant difference in our risk for heart attacks. The potentially hazardous behavior pattern of Type A can be altered by learning to think and plan differently.

Having a plan for a balanced lifestyle is important. Such a plan takes into account the need for work and play, for regular exercise, for diet control, for relaxation, and for building positive relationships. These things will help you reduce stress and improve your emotional—and physical—health.

The exercise on the following page will help you identify your own behavior patterns.

WHICH TYPE ARE YOU?

Listed below are 10 statements. Place a check (✓) in the column that is most descriptive of your behavior.

		Usually			Seldom	
1.	Do you move, walk, and eat rapidly?	1	2	3	4	5
2.	Do you feel impatient with the rate at which most events take place?	1	2	3	4	5
3.	Do you attempt to finish the sentences of persons speaking to you?	1	2	3	4	5
4.	Do you become irritated or even enraged when a car ahead of you in your lane runs at a pace you consider too slow?	1	2	3	4	5
5.	Do you find it uncomfortable to watch others perform tasks you know you can do faster?	1	2	3	4	5
6.	Do you find it difficult to be interested in others' conversations if the subject is not of special interest to you?	1	2	3	4	5
7.	Do you feel vaguely guilty when you do nothing for several hours or several days?	1	2	3	4	5
8.	Do you schedule more than is possible to accomplish in a given time span?	1	2	3	4	5
9.	Do you believe that whatever your success may be, it is because of your ability to get things done faster than others?	1	2	3	4	5
10.	Do you frequently clench your fist or bang your hand on the table to confirm your point during conversation?	1	2	3	4	5

Now add up your points. If your score is below 25, then you tend to be more like Type A. If it is above 25, then you tend to be more like Type B.

Meyer Friedman and Ray H. Rosenman, *Type A Behavior and Your Heart,* (New York: Fawcett Crest, 1974). Reproduced by permission.

The Three Stages of Stress

It is natural to resist or deny the presence of stress. We all have a tendency to "plow on," working harder and harder to overcome stressful situations rather than acknowledge the situation and "back off." In a stressful work environment, for example, a person may return to the office night after night trying to deal with the stress.

But there comes a point when the mind and the body simply become exhausted—stage 3 of stress. When this happens, efficiency decreases.

It is essential to learn to identify the stages of stress[*] before you get to exhaustion. If you continue to experience stress and do nothing to alter the situation, you are likely to develop physical problems. The three stages of stress are as follows:

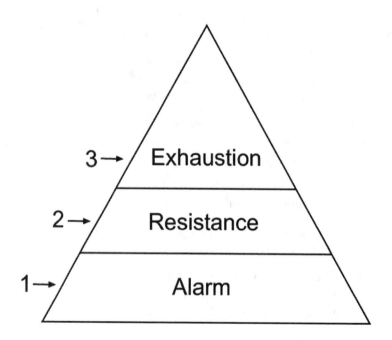

---

[*] Hans Selye, M.D., *The Stress of Life, rev. ed.* (New York: McGraw-Hill, 1976).

Identifying the Symptoms of Stress

The impact of stress usually can be reduced by identifying and accepting (owning) the feelings of stage 1 (alarm), avoiding the isolation and withdrawal of stage 2 (resistance), and seeking medical attention and/or psychological counseling for stage 3 (exhaustion). This section helps you see the symptoms at each stage so you can act on your stress and avoid moving into the next stage.

Alarm

Example: You discover that an expected promotion you had been promised and have already announced to friends is being held up for budget reasons.

Symptoms include:

Restlessness
Anxiety
Anger
Depression
Fear

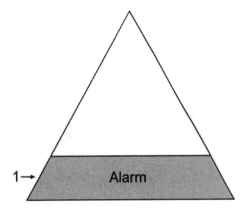

Resistance

Example: You resolve not to let anyone know about your disappointment.

Symptoms include:

Denial of Feelings
Emotional Isolation
Narrowing of Interests

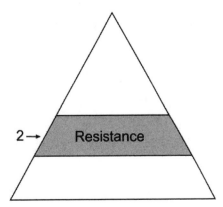

Exhaustion

Example: There is no change in your situation after several weeks—and you remain uncertain of whether you will ever receive the promotion.

Symptoms include:

Loss of Self-Confidence

Poor Sleep Habits

Unusual and Erratic Behavior

Physical Problems, such as
    Headaches
    Hypertension
    Abdominal Discomfort

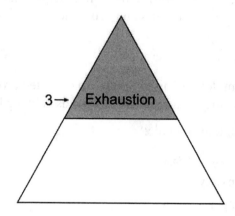

At each stage, taking a break (that is, doing something else or getting away from your work) is a helpful way to relieve stress. Sharing your situation with another caring person and talking out your feelings may help give a new perspective.

The Effect of Stress on the Physical Self

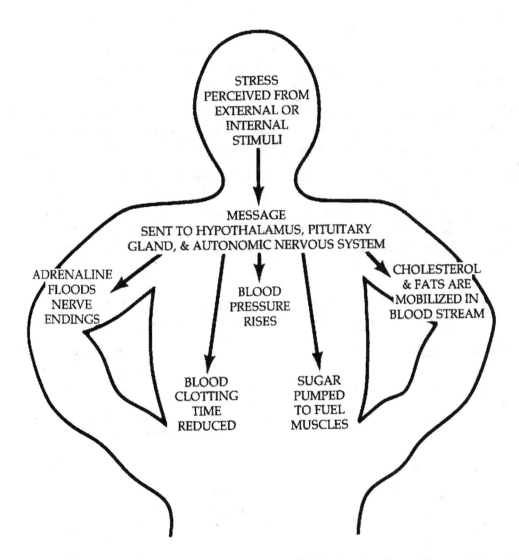

Continuous stress has been shown to have a gradual damaging effect on the cardio-vascular system, which can hasten the aging process.

Keeping the Adrenaline in Check

We have all heard stories of people being able to lift pianos and do other amazing feats under conditions of a house fire, automobile accident, and the like. Although that "high-voltage" charge of the hormone adrenaline in our system makes it possible to do incredible things, it also can be a kind of poison in the system if conditions stay at a peak indefinitely.

Yet it is possible to live in stressful situations over a relatively long period if you find ways to manage the stress. The diagram below suggests what happens as our system responds biochemically when we are under stress.

Our task is to find a way to restore our normal hormone balance. Finding our own best way to bring the stress level down regularly, and preferably daily, is both a challenge and a discipline. If we do not find that systematic way of bringing our stress level down to "normal," then our system tends to adjust to being at the "high-voltage" level. This then becomes destructive to both our physical and emotional systems.

Bloodstream Flooded with
"High-Voltage" Charge of Chemicals

System Under Stress: High Stress Level

System When Relaxed: Normal Level

System Returns to Normal
Hormone Balance

The goal is to return to a normal hormone level on a regular basis.

Examining Workplace Stress

Both supervisor and employees themselves play an important part in setting a climate for either creating or managing stress. We must recognize, however, that a certain amount of stress is necessary to get work done.

A supervisor needs to ask the question, "What do I do or what should I do to create a less stressful environment for my employees?" Some supervisors are referred to as "carriers of stress." This is analogous to a carrier of a virus that can be spread among the population.

As an employee, you need to ask the question, "What can or should I do to create a less stressful environment for myself and others?"

If we can accept the notion that "I stress me" (meaning I allow others to stress me), then we are willing and able to look at issues that help us so that we might determine how best to deal with stress in the workplace.

Occupational stress is prevalent in most work situations. Today, it is unrealistic to expect that jobs are stress-free. But if the organization's culture and the climate are such that both employer and employee are willing to work together in identifying stressful situations, stress can be minimized.

Symptoms of Stress in the Workplace

The symptoms below are particularly helpful in diagnosing stress in the workplace. Add any additional symptoms from your own experience.

1. When you face events with cynicism and negativism.

2. When the drive to pursue perfection pushes you beyond what is realistically possible.

3. When conflicts with your spouse and family seem to be increasing without clear reasons.

4. When alcohol and/or other drugs become an escape from the pressures of the job.

5. When you tend to bully and/or seek perfection from those you supervise.

6. When you have little time planned for anything except work.

7. When it seems impossible to relax or enjoy leisure activities because your mind is constantly on work.

8. When you feel ill at ease in social situations that are not related to work.

9. _____

10. _____

WHAT STRESSES YOU?

Listed below are seven job stressors. Look at the list and add an additional three stressors from your own work experience. Then rank all 10 in descending order to determine the areas of stress most pertinent to you.

_____   1. I am trapped in situations of conflict between people who expect different things of me.

_____   2. I am overloaded—they assign more than can be done (or) more than can be done well and maintain my self-esteem.

_____   3. I have ambiguous job responsibilities; I am not clear about the scope of my job.

_____   4. I am insecure about venturing outside my normal job boundaries.

_____   5. I have difficult supervisors (or subordinates).

_____   6. I worry over carrying responsibility for others.

_____   7. I lack participation in decisions affecting my job.

_____   8. _____

_____   9. _____

_____   10. _____

STRESS IN *YOUR* WORKPLACE

If you are a supervisor or manager, think about stress in your workplace and as honestly as you can, respond to the questions below.

1. What kinds of stress do you encounter as a consequence of your lifestyle?

   _____

   _____

   _____

   _____

2. What kinds of stress do those you supervise encounter as a result of your lifestyle?

   _____

   _____

   _____

   _____

3. What do you do that creates a climate for reducing or increasing stress in your work situation?

   _____

   _____

   _____

   _____

4. How aware are you of the kinds of stresses that employees bring with them from home?

   _____

   _____

   _____

   _____

Understanding Occupational Burnout

Is burnout a scientific diagnosis, an excuse, or a description of stressful conditions that have gone on too long?

Burnout is simply a description of the condition of people who have become discouraged or depressed or have developed a sense of hopelessness about being able to alleviate stress. Another way to think of burnout is as the logical conclusion over a long period of stress.

Conditions Leading to Burnout

➤ Unrealistically high expectations for yourself

➤ A sense of powerlessness in being able to remedy problems in the workplace

➤ Lack of support or encouragement from supervisors

➤ Preoccupation with work and putting in long hours to the exclusion of outside activities

Symptoms of Burnout

➤ Working long hours with an assumption that more time on the job will ease the stress

➤ Feeling exhaustion, fatigue, or muscle tension

➤ Dreading going to work each day

➤ Feeling a loss of appetite

➤ Being frequently ill

➤ Feeling bored and detached

➤ Being impatient and irritable with people at work and at home

➤ Having an inability to concentrate and a decreasing quality of work

➤ Expressing negative, cynical, and hostile attitudes toward others, particularly superiors

➤ Feeling a loss of self-esteem and self-confidence

➤ Blaming someone else when things go wrong

Who Is Most Likely to Experience Burnout?

➤ Administrators

➤ The "best" employees; dedicated workaholics

➤ Those in middle years of life—dealing with unfulfilled dreams, living up to others' expectations, disillusioned about what life is all about

➤ Those who feel "caught"—related to financial security, location changes, fear and/or the threat of unemployment

Dealing with Employee Burnout

Managers should strive to create a climate within the work situation in which:

➤ Negative feelings can be expressed

➤ Supervisors are provided training and support

➤ An opportunity is provided to understand employees as people

➤ It is possible to achieve realistic goals

➤ The reward system includes recognition for achievement

➤ Possibilities for staff realignment make it possible for job change, either temporarily or by way of promotion

➤ A career counseling program allows employees to talk about their own career goals

➤ A continuing education plan, which allows for new knowledge, training, and career redirection, is made a part of each employee's career objective

Finding the "Right" Amount of Stress

Although too much stress can have a negative personal impact, an appropriate amount of stress is an important part of being an effective person and employee. Without some stress, many of us would not bother to even get out of bed each morning. A certain amount of stress motivates us to achieve a standard of excellence that is a powerful step in promoting self-esteem. The goal is to find a level of stress that is helpful in producing good results without becoming debilitating.

The Yerkes-Dodson Law

The graph that follows shows the correlation between stress level and efficiency or performance. The bell curve of the Yerkes-Dodson Law[*] illustrates that efficiency and performance increase with the level of stress until a peak is reached. After that point, efficiency and performance steadily decline with more stress.

Yerkes-Dodson Law

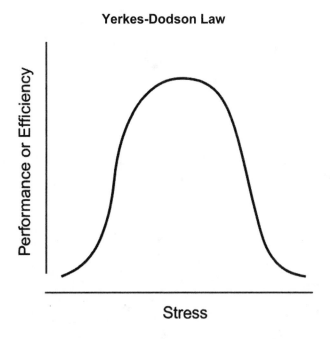

This emphasizes the need for everyone to find the stress level that is most effective for becoming quality individuals and quality employees. Optimum efficiency and optimum stress vary for everyone, so there is no "right" standard. Finding our ideal is an important dimension in being able to use the appropriate amount of stress in our lives.

---

[*] Herbert Benson and Robert Allen, "How Much Stress Is Too Much?" *Harvard Business Review,* (September/October, 1980). Copyright ©1980 by the President and Fellows of Harvard College; all rights reserved. Reprinted by permission.

Taking Responsibility for Your Own Stress

24

Identifying the Stress in Your Life

Besides major "life events" that we may experience from time to time, we also face stress from many "hassles" that occur routinely. These include events such as being stuck in traffic, meeting deadlines, having conflicts with family members, and generally dealing with busy lives. Between life events and day-to-day hassles, we are constantly faced with many stress-provoking situations.

Coping effectively requires an understanding of the situations we perceive to be stressful. What day-to-day hassles do you experience routinely?

Keeping a Weekly Stress Journal

The following activity will help you trace your stress levels to become more aware of the times, places, and circumstances that contribute to stress in your life. To keep the momentum in your writing, write no more than a brief paragraph for each day. Focus on who and what contributed to the stress and when and where it occurred for that particular day. Then rate your day on a scale of 1 to 10 (1 being little stress to 10 being high stress). Make copies of the form on the next page to trace your stress levels for as many weeks as you choose.

WEEKLY STRESS JOURNAL

Sunday

_____

_____

Monday

_____

_____

Tuesday

_____

_____

Wednesday

_____

_____

Thursday

_____

_____

Friday

_____

_____

Saturday

_____

_____

_____

CHARTING YOUR STRESS

As you keep your weekly stress journal, you will begin to see a pattern of where your stress is most significant. In this exercise, chart your stressors into the four main quadrants of home-family, work, recreation, and social life. Make notes in each quadrant of stressors related to each area of stress. Then pick the stressors out of all the items in all the quadrants that stand out as the most stressful to you. Think of the total, then rank the top eight stressors at the bottom of the page.

Stress Charting

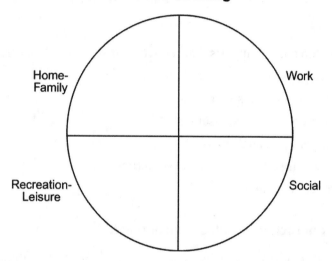

Home-Family

Work

Recreation-Leisure

Social

Rank in descending order all of the above stressors:

1. _____
2. _____
3. _____
4. _____
5. _____
6. _____
7. _____
8. _____

Coping with Stress

Book stores are filled with books on how to cope with stress. Each one offers its own perspective on stress along with various coping techniques. Coping is simply a way of short-circuiting the stress cycle—stopping the stress response.

There is no single right way of coping with a given situation. Consider the following ideas for figuring out what works best for you and for the stressors in your life.

Change your internal attitudes and perceptions.

Although you may not be able to change some types of external stimuli that are stressful, you can change your internal attitudes and perceptions of these stresses.

For example:

> ➤ Develop social supports that reduce your sense of aloneness
> ➤ Develop a sense of humor about your situation
> ➤ Talk about troubles with friends
> ➤ Seek professional counseling
> ➤ Own your personal stress
> ➤ Know yourself and your level of optimum stress
> ➤ Balance work and play

Change your interaction with the environment.

This strategy says that if you can "work smarter, not harder," you may be able to reduce your stress.

For example:

> ➤ Improve your skills in areas such as goal setting, time management and conflict management
> ➤ Take assertiveness training
> ➤ Use peer feedback to identify areas for possible changes in functioning
> ➤ Use a case consultant for particularly difficult job areas
> ➤ Slow down

Change your physical ability to cope.

The most common stress reduction activities are those designed to improve the physical resources of your body to handle the stress you experience.

For example:

> ➤ Get adequate and proper nutrition
> ➤ Start a fitness program
> ➤ Cut down on intake stressors (such as caffeine, nicotine, sugar)
> ➤ Relax and learn to loaf a little
> ➤ Get enough sleep and rest
> ➤ Develop recreational activities

Change your environment.

If a stressor is closely related to a particular environment, find a way to place yourself in a different environment. You should take caution, however, that you do not develop the habit of avoiding all stressful situations, but sometimes this may be a good short-term solution.

For example:

> ➤ Quit going to certain meetings
> ➤ Change job/vocation/location
> ➤ Develop extended education programs
> ➤ Structure time off from work
> ➤ Set up your job, if possible, so you can work in a variety of program areas

Alleviating Stress at Work

Developing good work habits can have a lot to do with your stress level on the job. The following are actions you can implement to help keep stress in check:

➤ Clarify organization mission and goals.

➤ Be orderly in work habits.

➤ Determine priorities and stick with them.

➤ Make a daily to-do list to keep on track; do not wait until the deadline.

➤ Stick with a decision once it is made. Do not continue to worry about whether you might have done better.

➤ Admit your mistakes; do not try to cover up. Do what you need to do to correct mistakes, and then get on with other tasks.

How Supervisors Can Help Employees Manage Stress

If you supervise others, then the stress level your employees experience on the job is partly a result of your actions and behaviors. The following guidelines will help you create a less stressful work environment:

➤ Outline goals clearly to workers and provide timely feedback on achievement.

➤ Be sure instructions are clear.

➤ Evaluate completion deadlines; are they reasonable?

➤ Eliminate conflict between your demands and other supervisors' demands.

➤ Deal with personality conflicts directly before they demoralize the rest of the group.

➤ Have regular work reviews to provide accurate and timely feedback.

➤ Reassure employees that good work is noted and appreciated.

➤ Have workers participate, as much as possible, in decisions that affect their work.

➤ Have a career development program that helps employees look at the reality of their job and the possibilities within their job situation.

➤ Have a well-functioning employee assistance program for recognizing and dealing with specific employee stressors.

Expressing Your Feelings

Perhaps the best way to relieve the pressure called stress is to express your feelings to caring individuals. Putting your feelings into words is often the key. This is in contrast to keeping feelings bottled up. Finding the best way to appropriately and constructively express your feelings is a useful learning experience.

Expressing your emotions can take many forms. Listed below are some constructive ideas. Review this list and place a check (✓) by those that fall within your comfort zone. Add your own stress relievers at the bottom of the list. Then rank in order the top five ways in which you prefer to express your feelings. Simply write the numbers 1 through 5 beside the box.

- ❑ Talk with your spouse or significant other.
- ❑ Talk with a good friend.
- ❑ Join a small sharing group.
- ❑ Use a tape recorder to verbalize feelings.
- ❑ Talk with a spiritual advisor, counselor, or therapist.
- ❑ Write letters to friends.
- ❑ Keep a journal describing your feelings.
- ❑ Talk with your supervisor at work.
- ❑ Have a family discussion.
- ❑ Exercise vigorously.
- ❑ _____
- ❑ _____
- ❑ _____
- ❑ _____
- ❑ _____

Using Stress Releases and Safety Valves

Part of stress management is simply recognizing where your stress is coming from, and another part is figuring out what you can do to release the stress and prevent it from building up to the breaking point. This is where the safety valve concept comes in—finding an outlet for pent-up energy or emotion.

How Do You Release Your Stress?

See how effective you are at using stress releases and safety valves to cope with stress. Rate yourself by placing a check (✓) in the column that best describes your use of each stress release or safety valve in the following list. Try to be completely honest.

I do well	I'm average	Need to improve	
5	**3**	**1**	**I'm succeeding at:**
_____	_____	_____	1. "Owning" my own stress—rather than blaming others
_____	_____	_____	2. Knowing my level of optimum stress—the level at which I am doing my best without becoming destructive
_____	_____	_____	3. Balancing work and play—allowing time for both
_____	_____	_____	4. Loafing more—doing nothing at times and feeling okay about it
_____	_____	_____	5. Getting enough sleep and rest rather than ending up with what is left over at the end of the day
_____	_____	_____	6. Refusing to take on more than I can handle—learning to say "no"
_____	_____	_____	7. Working off tension—engaging in hard physical effort on a regular basis
_____	_____	_____	8. Setting realistic goals—those that can be achieved within a reasonable time frame
_____	_____	_____	9. Practicing relaxation, such as meditating with music or biofeedback

I do well	I'm average	Need to improve	
_____	_____	_____	10. Slowing down—taking pleasure in every moment rather than rushing through life
_____	_____	_____	11. Putting emphasis on *being* rather than on *doing*—*being* a person others like to be around rather than just *doing* many activities
_____	_____	_____	12. Managing my time, including planning for time alone—setting priorities and doing those things that are most important
_____	_____	_____	13. Planning regular recreation—a complete change of pace and something that is fun to do
_____	_____	_____	14. Following a physical fitness program
_____	_____	_____	15. Avoiding too much caffeine
_____	_____	_____	16. Emphasizing good nutrition in my diet
_____	_____	_____	17. Avoiding alcohol or other chemicals to deal with pressure—alcohol and drug dependency relieves symptoms without addressing the problem
_____	_____	_____	18. Avoiding emotional "overload"—taking on others' problems when you are already under stress
_____	_____	_____	19. Selecting emotional "investments" more carefully—things that call for emotional involvement
_____	_____	_____	20. Giving and accepting positive "strokes"
_____	_____	_____	21. Talking out troubles and getting professional help if needed—being willing to seek help is a sign of strength rather than weakness

Total checks in each column

Multiply:

x 5	x 3	x 1
_____	_____	_____

TOTAL SCORE

Score Yourself

If you scored between 21 and 50, then you need to develop several areas to better release your stress. Discuss some of your answers with a counselor or close friend.

If you scored between 51 and 75, you have discovered a variety of ways to deal effectively with stress. Make a note of those items you checked "need to improve" and work on strategies to help you move to the "I'm Average" box.

If your score was 75 or greater—congratulations! You apparently have found excellent ways to deal with frustration and the complexities of life. Stay alert to protect the valuable skills you have acquired.

Review this book later and rate yourself again.

Refer to this list after you review the case study on the following page. You will have the opportunity to assess Maria's stressful situation and recommend stress releases and safety valves for her.

CASE STUDY: Maria's Overwhelming Stress

Maria is a single mother of two young children who works full time as a legal secretary in a well-known law firm. Following her divorce, Maria went back to school to acquire skills for a job that would pay enough to support herself and her children.

Maria's daily routine seems increasingly overwhelming. She gets up at 5:30 A.M. to prepare breakfast, make lunches, and do laundry. At 7:30 she drops Jose, age 2, at the babysitter and takes daughter Carla, age 7, to school. (Carla's school is 10 miles in the opposite direction from where Maria works.)

At work, Maria is expected to be on time and to deliver high-quality output. Yet it is difficult for her to get to work on time when there are even simple problems with the children. When they are sick, Maria feels the need to take time off. Her supervisor is very demanding, and when he is under pressure, he expects her to work overtime or take work home.

To compound things, Maria has been taking an advanced course in computer skills two nights a week to prepare for a better job and improve her financial position as the children get older. The course work adds to her stress.

In summary, Maria's day is filled with stress from morning until she goes to bed at night. She has little time for herself and does not see much hope for change in the next several years.

What is likely to happen if nothing changes this picture? What safety valves would you suggest?

_____

_____

_____

_____

_____

_____

Compare your responses to the authors' suggestions in the Appendix.

36

Reducing Stress Through Biofeedback, Mindfulness, and Meditation

Understanding Biofeedback

Researchers had long speculated that human beings' emotional attitudes and thought processes had a direct impact on their physical and emotional health. And now *biofeedback*—making unconscious or involuntary bodily processes perceptible to the senses so they can be manipulated by conscious mental control—is well established in the psychological and medical communities.

Indeed, we can learn to control any physiological process—such as brain waves, temperature, and pulse—that we can measure and observe by biofeedback. With scientific instruments, we are able to observe and measure how our thoughts and emotions cause changes in body physiology.

For example, by learning to quiet our thoughts through biofeedback training, we can significantly increase our blood flow to warm our hands. Likewise, quieting the mind and learning to focus our thoughts also can reduce stress responses.

Developing Mindfulness

Mindfulness is developing internal awareness, acceptance, and equanimity. Put another way, mindfulness is focusing on present-moment experiences rather than on thoughts of the past or future. Simply being "in the moment" results in calmness and contentment. This strengthens our resilience to stress.

Discontinuing Judgmental Behavior

A basic step in becoming mindful is learning not to judge ourselves and others. Constantly judging ourselves and others, usually negatively, is a common way of contributing to stress. By blaming ourselves for "human error," we are constantly adding to our stress level as it becomes more apparent that we will never be able to overcome our human qualities.

A nonjudgmental attitude is a significant ingredient to reducing stress. Forgiveness of self and others—and genuine acceptance of self and others—are keys to reducing powerful negative internal forces. These forces can lead to stress and often contribute to physical illness. By practicing mindfulness techniques we can learn to "slow down the system" in such a way that also may reduce the stressors that can lead to physical and mental illness.

Refraining from Multitasking

Being mindful "in the moment" is a skill of mindfulness training, focusing your attention on only one thing at a time. In typical American culture we pride ourselves on doing many tasks at the same time. Reading while shaving or watching TV is one example. Another example is speaking on a cell phone while driving the car or cooking dinner. Having several projects going at the same time often contributes to moving from one to another without a sense of accomplishment about any of them.

A multitasking pattern adds to stress, even though we often feel we are being efficient by taking on many tasks at once. In contrast to what we might expect, multitasking has been shown to reduce efficiency, causing us to end up accomplishing less.

Practicing Meditation

Busy, overactive lives frequently contribute to overwhelming stress. Thus, slowing down our lives is a way to lessen stress. Yoga is one way to slowly, gently, and mindfully listen to our bodies. Another way is regularly practicing mindfulness meditation.

The pages that follow outline six easy but basic meditation exercises[*] that can make a difference in your life:

> **Breathing Meditation**—Mindfulness of breathing is a basic dimension of meditation practice. Because breathing is so much a part of us, this meditation, if used regularly, soon becomes a powerful ally in stress management.

> **Raisin Meditation**—To reduce any feelings that meditation is somehow unusual or mystical, the raisin exercise helps illustrate meditation and mindfulness in a down-to-earth way.

> **Walking Meditation**—A simple way of bringing awareness into your life is to practice meditation for 30 minutes while walking because walking is an activity that most of us do daily.

> **Listening to Music Meditation**—All kinds of music affect our lives each day. This exercise helps you focus on this audio stimulation as a way of developing awareness.

> **Body Awareness Meditation**—We sometimes support and maintain our physical selves and sometimes abuse and destroy our physical bodies. It is easy to live our lives without being focused on the many body parts it takes to function in a healthy way as a total body—unless, that is, we become sick or injured. This exercise heightens your awareness of all parts of your body.

> **"Wise Person" Meditation**—We face problems and choices almost daily. For some people, this is extremely stressful because they feel great concern for the potential consequences. For others, problem solving and making choices are made easily with little concern for the consequences. This exercise helps you tune in to your intuition for guidance.

---

[*] Jon Kabat-Zinn, *Full Catastrophe Living,* (New York: Dell Publishing Group, ©1990).

BREATHING MEDITATION

Taking only 15 minutes, this exercise can be used any time throughout the day, whether you are sitting or standing.

Step 1: Assume a comfortable position either lying on your back or sitting.

Step 2: Now...close your eyes (if comfortable).

Step 3: Now...bring attention to your abdomen, and notice the rise and fall of your breathing.

Step 4: Now...focus on your breathing, staying focused on each in-breath and on each out-breath.

Step 5: Now...every time your mind wanders away from the focus on breathing, notice what it was that took you away and then gently bring your attention back to your breathing.

Step 6: If you find your mind wandering repeatedly, simply bring it back to your breathing repeatedly.

Step 7: Practice this exercise for 15 minutes every day for one week, in a disciplined way, before evaluating what this practice can mean for you. Become aware of what it means to "spend time" with your breath each day. This shifts your focus from the cares of the day.

RAISIN MEDITATION[*]

This exercise brings focus to eating, which is often done rapidly with little awareness of its meaning in our lives.

Step 1: Select three raisins at random.

Step 2: Now…take one raisin, observing it carefully as if you have never seen it before. Feel its texture and notice its color and surfaces.

Step 3: Now…be aware of any previous thoughts about raisins or food in general.

Step 4: Now…smell the raisin, with increased awareness.

Step 5: Now…bring the raisin to your lips, being aware of your hand and arm motion and your anticipation (salivating) of eating the raisin.

Step 6: Now…put the raisin in your mouth and chew it slowly, fully experiencing the taste of one raisin.

Step 7: Now…when ready to swallow, experience the process fully, imagining how your body is one raisin heavier.

Step 8: Now…repeat with the second raisin, and then the third.

[*] From *Full Catastrophe Living* by Jon Kabat-Zinn, copyright ©1990 by Jon Kabat-Zinn. Used by permission of Dell Publishing, a division of Random House, Inc.

3: Reducing Stress Through Biofeedback, Mindfulness, and Meditation

WALKING MEDITATION[*]

This exercise brings your attention to walking, which we tend to take for granted. (If you use a wheelchair, focus on the movement of the wheels and the sensations of rolling over bumps or negotiating difficult passageways.)

Step 1: In beginning to walk, be fully aware of how one foot contacts the ground weight shifts from one foot to the next as each foot makes contact with the ground in turn.

Step 2: Now...when your mind wanders away from attention to your feet or legs, simply bring your attention back as you become aware of it.

Step 3: Now...to concentrate, do not look around at the sights but instead, keep focused in front.

Step 4: Now...stay looking ahead rather than looking down at your feet. Be aware of the balancing that occurs.

Step 5: Now...become fully aware of the sensations of walking—nothing more.

---

[*] From *Full Catastrophe Living* by Jon Kabat-Zinn, copyright ©1990 by Jon Kabat-Zinn. Used by permission of Dell Publishing, a division of Random House, Inc.

LISTENING TO MUSIC MEDITATION[*]

For this exercise, any kind of music can be useful. Do not judge the music on whether it is "good" or "bad." This exercise is to experience music, not to critique it. Listen only; do not be distracted. If you are distracted, simply let your thoughts come back to the music.

Step 1: Select any music (15 minutes' worth)

Step 2: Now…listen carefully, noticing the rhythm.

Step 3: Now…listen carefully, noticing the tune.

Step 4: Now…listen carefully, noticing changes in the music.

Step 5: Now…listen carefully, noticing the words (if any).

Step 6: Now…listen carefully, noticing the emotion(s) the music brings to your awareness.

Step 7: Now…listen carefully, noticing the thoughts the music brings to your awareness.

[*] From *Full Catastrophe Living* by Jon Kabat-Zinn, copyright ©1990 by Jon Kabat-Zinn. Used by permission of Dell Publishing, a division of Random House, Inc.

BODY AWARENESS MEDITATION[*]

This exercise focuses on your body—increasing self-awareness and relaxation as a meditative experience. While you are doing this exercise, notice any sensations, feelings, tensions, or discomforts including pain.

Step 1: Find a comfortable lying-down position with minimum strictures and close your eyes.

Step 2: Now focus on your breathing. Notice your abdomen expand and contract.

Step 3: Now focus on your toes (first right foot, then left) and relax them.

Now focus on your feet (first right foot, then left) and relax them.

Now focus on your calves and legs (first right leg, then left) and relax them.

Now focus on your thighs (first right thigh, then left) and relax them.

Now focus on your buttocks (first right buttock, then left) and relax them.

Now focus on hip area (first right hip, then left) and relax them.

Now focus on your stomach/abdomen and relax.

Now focus on your chest area and relax it.

Now focus on your shoulders (first right shoulder, then left) and relax them.

Now focus on your arms (first right arm, then left) and relax them.

Now focus on your hands (first right hand, then left) and relax them.

Now focus on your fingers (first on right hand, then the left) and relax them.

Now focus on your neck and relax it.

Now focus on your face muscles and relax them.

Now focus on forehead and top of head and relax them.

Step 4: Focus on the top of your head. Imagine air coming up from your feet all the way to the top of your head and rushing out the top of your head and back through to your feet and then back through the top of your head again. Then visualize the air going back and forth from head to feet.

---

[*] From *Full Catastrophe Living* by Jon Kabat-Zinn, copyright ©1990 by Jon Kabat-Zinn. Used by permission of Dell Publishing, a division of Random House, Inc.

"WISE PERSON" VISUALIZATION

This visualization exercise is intended to help you focus on your intuitive self in finding guidance for making decisions.

Step 1:   Find a comfortable position with a minimum of constrictions.

Step 2:   Now close your eyes.

Step 3:   Now envision a warm, comfortable day with plans to climb a steep and difficult mountain.

Step 4:   Now envision yourself climbing the mountain. Notice the leg muscle strain in climbing. Notice the warmth of the sun. Notice the rocks you need to climb over. Notice the brambles you need to avoid.

Step 5:   Now envision being tired and sweaty as you climb. Notice your decision to sit down to rest on a large boulder. Envision the need for rest and a drink of water.

Step 6:   Now envision finally getting to the top of the mountain, again experiencing all of the discomforts noted above.

Step 7:   Now envision unexpectedly meeting a person at the top of the mountain. Envision sitting down with this person. You recognize this person as very wise. In your mind who is this person?

Step 8:   Now, after introductory conversation, envision asking this person the following question: "What's the most important thing I should be doing right now?" and/or "What should I do now to solve the problem I am facing or decision I am needing to make?"

Step 9:   Now after receiving the answer from this wise person, you start down the mountain.

Step 10: Now be aware of your feelings as you go back down the mountain.

How committed are you to following the advice you heard from the "wise person"?

SEVEN ATTITUDES THAT CONTRIBUTE TO EMOTIONAL HEALTH*

For the following seven attitudes, circle the number that indicates how you see yourself, with 1 meaning you have a low recognition of this attitude and 10 meaning a high recognition.

1. Recognition that everything is connected: All people are part of the universal family. Accepting all people of different races and cultures is the opposite of being judgmental and prejudicial toward people who are different from ourselves.

   1   2   3   4   5   6   7   8   9   10

2. Recognition that relationships are important and need constant maintenance: Marriage or companionships, professional relationships, and other significant relationships all need careful nurturing and mindful respect. Building friendships is like investing in our immediate health as well as investing in our future well-being.

   1   2   3   4   5   6   7   8   9   10

3. Recognition that it is important to respect and care for ourselves: Self-respect and self-esteem are also important for maintaining good emotional health and for maintaining a healthy physical body.

   1   2   3   4   5   6   7   8   9   10

4. Recognition that love is a key ingredient leading to survival and the ability to thrive: Forgiving ourselves and forgiving others is symbolic of a loving attitude. The opposite of this attitude is one of vengeance and manipulation.

   1   2   3   4   5   6   7   8   9   10

CONTINUED

CONTINUED

5. Recognition that spirituality in our lives allows us to connect with the universe: Being open to a higher power is sometimes the key to finding relief after struggling with pain and failure from trying to "do it alone."

   1   2   3   4   5   6   7   8   9   10

6. Recognition of the importance of seeking truth rather than being blinded by biases and prejudices: This allows us to let go of perceptions and stereotypes that are untrue and to become nonjudgmental in our dealings with others.

   1   2   3   4   5   6   7   8   9   10

7. Recognition that living in the moment helps us to be focused and "present" with ourselves and others: This means letting go of the past and reducing our preoccupation with the future. A daily 10–15 minute mindfulness meditation encourages living in the present.

   1   2   3   4   5   6   7   8   9   10

---

[*] From *Anatomy of the Spirit* by Caroline Myss, Ph.D., copyright ©1996 by Caroline Myss. Used by permission of Harmony Books, a division of Random House, Inc.

Native American Attitudes Toward Being and Becoming

Show Respect to Others	–	Every Person Has a Special Gift
Share What You Have	–	Giving Makes You Richer
Know Who You Are	–	You Are a Reflection on Your Family
Accept What Life Brings	–	You Cannot Control Many Things
Have Patience	–	Some Things Cannot Be Rushed
Live Carefully	–	What You Do Will Come Back to You
Take Care of Others	–	You Cannot Live Without Them
Honor Your Elders	–	They Show You the Way of Life
Pray for Guidance	–	Many Things Are Not Known
See Connections	–	All Things Are Related

(Posted on bulletin board at Haskell Indian Nations University, Lawrence, Kansas)

Improving Relationships with Self and Others

Accepting Yourself as a Unique Individual

Understanding and accepting *yourself* is the first step toward relating successfully to others. In this competitive world there is often pressure to "be like somebody else." We may have grown up with the feeling that we are not acceptable the way we are. If prolonged, these feelings can develop into a poor self-image.

Those who have a difficult time accepting themselves often project their underlying feelings of personal unworthiness to others. So they develop a distorted assumption that friends and family do not like them. A significant event in counseling is when these individuals become aware that it is *they* who do not like or accept themselves.

When you identify your uniqueness and are willing to enhance or modify your good qualities, you are on the right track.

How Are You Unique?

The following exercise will help you identify your unique qualities. In the first block below, list the names of individuals you see as being similar to you and make a note of the similarities. In block #2, list traits of those same individuals that you see as different from you, and state in what ways they are different. Finally, identify three characteristics that are uniquely you (block #3) and briefly describe how each characteristic is or can be an asset to your future development.

#1 Similar

1. _____
   name   ways similar

2. _____

3. _____

#2 Different

1. _____
   name   ways different

2. _____

3. _____

#3 Uniquely Me

1. _____
   characteristic   why an asset

2. _____

3. _____

In what ways can my uniqueness become an asset?

_____

_____

_____

Sorting Realistic from Unrealistic Expectations

False assumptions about people can produce unrealistic expectations. Sorting out what is realistic and unrealistic is an important part of growth. For example, some people are more sensitive than others and become depressed when criticized or if there is any indication that they are not appreciated by everyone. This is an example of a false assumption that can lead to emotional stress. In reality, no matter what kind of contribution a person is making, not everyone will appreciate that contribution equally.

Listed below are 10 false assumptions that work against understanding ourselves and our relationships with others:

1. That it is possible for everybody to like us

2. That we must be competent and adequate all of the time

3. That other people are bad if they do not share our values

4. That "all is lost" when we get treated unfairly or experience rejection

5. That we cannot control or change our feelings

6. That unless everything is structured and understandable, there is reason to be fearful or anxious

7. That problems of the past that have influenced our lives must continue to determine our feelings and behavior

8. That it is easier to avoid problems than to accept them and begin working toward a solution

9. That life should be better than it is

10. That health and happiness can be realized by waiting for somebody else to make something happen

Do any of these sound familiar? On the lines that follow, write a brief statement about any of the 10 that have caused you the most difficulty.

_____

_____

_____

_____

_____

Assessing Your Strengths

We have more strengths than we often realize. Others may see strengths in us that we minimize or do not recognize at all. Moreover, some incongruity often exists between what we feel is a strength and what we perceive that others feel.

People who underestimate their strengths, for example, often cannot accept praise without needing to negate it in some way. These same people are not likely to accept a challenging assignment because of an underlying fear that they are not capable and would not do a satisfactory job.

Assess your own strengths by writing brief statements about the following. Be as realistic and honest as possible.

Things I feel I do well:

_____

_____

_____

_____

_____

_____

Things other people consider as my strengths:

_____

_____

_____

_____

_____

_____

Things I can do for others to help them recognize and realize their strengths:

_____

_____

_____

_____

_____

_____

Acknowledging Universal Human Needs

Understanding the basic needs of others helps us understand how to better relate to them. Human relationships are developed when people freely give to and receive from one another. Relationships in which only one person's needs are being met tend to be shallow and short-lived.

Knowing that others need to feel important, to be appreciated, and to have others interested in them is essential to building good human relationships. Having their needs met helps people stay emotionally healthy.

What follows is a list of universal human needs. Add to this list any of your own needs that are missing and then rank them in order, with 1 being your most important need.

Rank

_____ The need to feel important to oneself and in the eyes of others

_____ The need to be perceived as successful by self and others

_____ The need to be needed and/or wanted

_____ The need to feel useful

_____ The need to be loved, appreciated, accepted, and/or recognized by others

_____ The need to feel influential

_____ The need to belong to something bigger than oneself

_____ The need to grow in skills or learning

_____ The need for adventure

Others:

_____ _____

_____ _____

_____ _____

_____ _____

Building Better Relationships

Interacting with people can be either a positive experience that produces good feelings or a negative experience that produces bad feelings.

The ability to build warm and supportive relationships, while maintaining integrity or identity, is essential to emotional health. Being able to say, "I disagree with you but will explore other alternatives," is a healthy approach.

Being aware of how we relate to family and friends is an important first step toward having positive relationships. In the exercise that follows, circle the number that best represents the way you relate to others.

I don't listen to what is really being said.	1	2	3	4	5	I listen with genuine interest.
I cut people off in conversation.	1	2	3	4	5	I let people finish before jumping in with my thoughts.
I make judgments about people before getting to know them.	1	2	3	4	5	I do not let first impressions determine a relationship.
I am not interested in other people's problems or ideas.	1	2	3	4	5	I devote attention to other people before rushing in to talk about myself.
I have no interest in the success of others.	1	2	3	4	5	I can honestly compliment and encourage the success of others.
I am unable to tolerate joking and kidding by others.	1	2	3	4	5	I am able to enjoy all forms of humor.
I discourage opinions that differ from my own.	1	2	3	4	5	I respond to new ideas with enthusiasm.
I show impatience with others in nonverbal ways that express disapproval.	1	2	3	4	5	My body language shows approval of others.

If you have more 1s and 2s than 4s and 5s, this may be an indication that you need additional work in learning to work with others.

Recognizing Negative Relationship Patterns

Frequently we get into patterns of relating that are not satisfying, yet we are unable to change a pattern because it is so much a part of us. Poor interpersonal habits are like old friends—they are hard to give up.

Recognizing that we can change patterns that have brought us difficulties in the past is the next step toward positive personal relationships. What follows are interpersonal relationship patterns to be avoided:

> ➢ **Placing people automatically in "boxes"**—This does not allow much opportunity to get to know a person as a unique individual. For example, you may think, "I do not like Alice because she lives in a poor part of town." You have put Alice in a negative box without relating to her as a person.

> ➢ **Being combative**—Relationships often become strained when the individuals tend to be argumentative and rigid. Although some people enjoy arguing, most do not. If you set up disagreements in your conversations, people will learn to avoid you rather than enter a contest of wills every time they talk with you.

> ➢ **Being too agreeable**—When this happens, you seem not to have unique qualities. If you tend to be all smiles and without an opinion, even when you disagree on a serious subject, others will discredit your willingness to speak your feelings and may begin to distrust you.

What Is Your Pattern?

Which of the above most closely resembles you? Jot your response below, and explain your reasons. Are there any other negative patterns in your "interpersonal style"?

_____

_____

_____

_____

_____

Becoming more aware of yourself helps you to understand why relationships are sometimes difficult. Accepting responsibility for conflicts and interpersonal problems is an important step toward positive change.

HOW WELL DO YOU RELATE TO OTHERS?

Emotional health is often determined by the way people work with and relate to others. This exercise will enable you to assess your style of relating to others. Be as honest as you can.

Others would say that I:

	Usually	Occasionally	Seldom
1. Communicate easily and clearly with people	_____	_____	_____
2. Am a good listener	_____	_____	_____
3. Communicate assertively without being critical or negative	_____	_____	_____
4. Relate to others with self-confidence	_____	_____	_____
5. Discuss feelings with others	_____	_____	_____
6. Face conflict and handle antagonism	_____	_____	_____
7. Resolve interpersonal problems between myself and others	_____	_____	_____
8. Accept expressions of warmth from friends	_____	_____	_____
9. Trust other people	_____	_____	_____
10. Influence my peers constructively	_____	_____	_____

CONTINUED

	Usually	Occasionally	Seldom
11. Assume responsibility for difficulties with others	_____	_____	_____
12. Discuss important issues with an open mind	_____	_____	_____
13. Encourage feedback from others about my behavior	_____	_____	_____
14. Am relatively free of prejudice	_____	_____	_____
15. Am open and easy to get to know	_____	_____	_____

If you answered "usually" to 10 of the above, you appear to have good relationships with others. If you answered "occasionally" to five or more, you may need to focus more on this area. If you answered "seldom" to any question, then this is an excellent place to begin working on self-improvement.

CASE STUDY: John Relates to Family and Friends

John, age 37, is a construction worker. He and his wife, Shirley, have four children, the youngest of whom is a high school junior.

John frequently has conflicts on the job and at home. He does not know why he becomes involved with other people to the point of getting into an argument. He often winds up alienating people who could be his friends. He feels upset with himself after arguing with his wife or family members when they try to communicate with him.

John is vaguely aware that he has not been promoted because of his inability to get along with co-workers. And his wife recently threatened him with divorce after an especially intense argument. His relationship with his children, which has never been strong, has deteriorated. His family views him as extremely judgmental and critical. To avoid constant arguments, his family and friends tend to stay away from him.

John has difficulty understanding himself and even more difficulty understanding his trouble getting along with others. Things have reached a point that he genuinely wants help to correct some of his problems.

What do you think are his chances for significant change? What suggestions would you make?

_____

_____

_____

_____

_____

_____

Compare your responses to the authors' suggestions in the Appendix.

Enhancing Your
Emotional Health

Understanding Emotional Maturity

In its simplest form, emotional health is the capacity to work (be productive), to love (have friends), and to play (renew oneself) with relative freedom from internal stress and without causing stress to others. In another sense, emotional health is the capacity to cope with all of life, including its joys and sorrows—what could be termed *emotional maturity.*[*]

Do you consider yourself emotionally healthy? The following are criteria that describe an emotionally mature person. Place a check (✓) by those statements that you feel describe you.

Emotionally mature individuals:

_____ 1. Experience fully the entire range of human emotions

_____ 2. Develop and maintain satisfying relationships with others

_____ 3. See life as a learning experience that can bring rewards from experience

_____ 4. Are free from debilitating fears that unduly restrict risk taking

_____ 5. Accept unchangeable reality and make the most of the situation

_____ 6. Accept themselves in a realistic way

_____ 7. Are relatively free from prejudice and accept differences in others

_____ 8. Assume personal responsibility without blaming others

_____ 9. Accept emotional support from others and appropriately express feelings that give support to others

_____ 10. Rebound from crises without prolonged feelings of stress, grief, or guilt

If you checked five or more items, you are on your way to emotional maturity. None of us ever achieves total maturity, so do not be discouraged if you did not check all 10 statements. Understand that life is an opportunity to learn and grow.

---

[*] For an excellent book on this subject, read *Emotional Intelligence Works* by S. Michael Kravitz and Susan Schubert, Thomson Learning/Course Technology.

Expressing Emotions Appropriately

The ability to experience and express emotions is uniquely human. Fear, anger, joy, grief, jealousy, love, anxiety, and depression are common human emotions.

Our emotional makeup is that part of us that contributes to the elation of great joy or the depths of profound sorrow. Emotions also warn us of danger and give us a way to express and receive love and affection as well as anger and sorrow.

The emotionally mature person learns to express these emotions appropriately. Emotional maturity also contributes to the ability to maintain evenness through the ups and downs of life without the demands of continual extreme highs or lows.

Perils of Pent-up Emotions

Emotional health or illness is far more complex than the physical. When we get physically sick, most of us visit a medical doctor. The doctor prescribes treatment that usually alleviates the problem. Thus, physical illness has a fairly direct relationship between symptom and treatment or cure.

With emotional difficulties, however, the relationship between symptom and treatment is often much less direct. Some people may not even acknowledge their symptoms. Many people, for example, have been taught not to show their emotions. Some have learned that they should not even have emotions (feelings) about certain events. Males in particular have frequently received messages from parents or society that "real men" should strictly control their emotions. The assumption is that it is better to deal with the world on the basis of logic rather than feelings.

Emotions are the feelings associated with all of the events and activities in our lives. For example, most people feel grief when a loved one dies. These feelings are normal and when experienced fully, they allow the mourner to adapt to the loss. People who do not know how to experience these feelings satisfactorily may be overtaken by despair. Rather than healing from their sense of loss, these people may develop depression that becomes chronic and incapacitating.

Children who are physically or sexually abused often carry the scars and stigma of such experiences into adult life. These "scars" affect their capacity to express feelings to others as well as to receive feelings in return. Often a layer of guilt, although unfounded, is part of the complex emotional problems that persist into adulthood.

All of us deal with our emotions either destructively or constructively. For some, bottling up of emotions may result in physical problems. For others, the expression of emotions may be inappropriate for the time or situation and result in negative feedback.

CASE STUDY: Roger Deals with a Common Problem

Roger is a young man who recently completed college. He selected a major he liked and his grades were above average. By all of the usual standards he should be a happy person. As the youngest member of a high-achieving family (where all members have become successful), Roger feels considerable pressure to succeed. Roger is also contemplating marriage to his longtime girlfriend and this has increased the pressure.

Roger sometimes feels overwhelmed about the future. Recently, he has been spending more and more time alone. His friends are starting to see him as preoccupied and moody. For the first time in his life, he finds it difficult to make decisions about the future.

Although he feels that his future would be difficult to discuss with friends, Roger is worried about his family's high expectations. He is uneasy that he will not measure up to the success of his brothers and sisters. Now that the college routine is over, he is unsettled about the future and his lack of structure.

Unfortunately, Roger has been conditioned to think that real men do not express their feelings. He has approached his present situation by trying not to let anybody know how he is feeling inside. In fact, much of the time he is not sure what he is feeling. He is spending more and more time alone.

What is likely to happen to Roger's behavior and feelings if he does not find a way to come out of his shell?

_____

_____

_____

_____

_____

_____

Compare your responses to the authors' suggestions in the Appendix.

Exploring Your Own Emotional Fitness

One of the most difficult aspects of developing and maintaining emotional health is being able to look at oneself objectively. A necessary first step is exploring your feelings about yourself and how you relate to others. Learning about yourself can be an exciting adventure or journey. Each discovery can open up new possibilities for growth. As you learn more about yourself, you may learn to realistically accept limitations or begin to see previously unrecognized potential.

Everyone has a combination of emotions, attitudes, and behaviors that creates a unique personality. You have considerable control over the pieces that make up your personality. Learning to maximize your potential, once it is discovered, is what makes life challenging and exciting.

Examining Your Approach to Life

The exercise that follows is an opportunity to review how well you understand key issues related to emotional health. Do not worry if the questions seem new or strange or if you have difficulty with the answers.

Being as honest as you can, circle the answer that best describes you.

My friends would agree that:

1.	I am basically a pessimistic person.	True	False
2.	I often wish I were somebody else or had another person's qualities.	True	False
3.	I often find myself angry at people.	True	False
4.	I tend to blame others for my problems.	True	False
5.	I often assume blame for other people's problems.	True	False
6.	I find it difficult to encourage and support others' successes.	True	False
7.	It is hard for me to accept encouragement and support from friends or family.	True	False
8.	I do not have many friends.	True	False
9.	I worry constantly about things I cannot change.	True	False
10.	I am frightened about things that others do not seem concerned about.	True	False

If you answered true to five or more statements, now is a good time to review your approach to life.

Building Self-Confidence

Without self-confidence you can find yourself in a vicious circle: Self-confidence is required to plan for the future, to go forth and make your mark; but if you lack self-confidence, you may develop a fear of the future. This, in turn, will inhibit the building of self-confidence because confidence comes from success. And then you will be right back where you started—with a lack of self-confidence that makes you fear the future.

How can you get out of this circle?

Taking *action* is the key. Confidence is not automatic. It does not come because we wish to have it. It comes from experiencing success. Self-confidence must be built and nurtured.

Pitfalls on the Path to Self-Confidence

All of us experience failures. These can tend to destroy our confidence. Thus, dwelling on our failures and forgetting our past successes can lead us to develop a fear of the future.

Another way to destroy self-confidence is to compare ourselves to others. There is always someone more capable than we are—even within our areas of strength. Constantly making comparisons can unintentionally lead to a decrease in self-confidence.

Being governed by the need to gain others' approval also will make achieving self-confidence difficult. Finding our own uniqueness and then building on it is a key ingredient of self-confidence.

Listed below is a series of "starts" and "stops" that can help you build self-confidence. Check (✓) those that you feel you need to give more attention to.

- ❑ Start liking myself
- ❑ Stop running myself down
- ❑ Stop comparing myself to others
- ❑ Start making full use of my abilities
- ❑ Start viewing mistakes as a way to learn
- ❑ Start remembering past successes
- ❑ Start becoming an "expert" at my present job
- ❑ Start finding areas in my life in which I can make positive changes
- ❑ Start initiating a self-improvement program
- ❑ Start taking action rather than just planning to take action

Solving Problems Openly

Problem solving is an important skill in dealing with interpersonal conflict. Improving your relationships depends on your being open to discussion and change, rather than storing resentments.

Steps to Achieving Openness

The following steps will help you learn to be more open in your relationships with others:

> **Intent**—Openness with others must come from a genuine desire to improve the relationship rather than to win arguments. Caring about others will increase the likelihood of your being taken seriously, even when you disagree.

> **Mutuality**—Try for a shared understanding of your relationship. You need to know how others perceive your behavior, as well as how to communicate your understanding of their behavior.

> **Risk Taking**—Your willingness to risk depends on the importance you place on the relationship because any effort at openness involves a degree of risk. You need to anticipate a potential loss of some self-esteem. Being rejected or hurt by another is always a possibility. The important thing is being willing to risk letting the other person react naturally when working through interpersonal problems.

> **Lack of Coercion**—When discussion between you and others becomes emotional, this should not become a tool to get others to change their behavior. Instead, the discussion should be about clarifying the situation. The purpose should be to determine what can be learned from the discussion that will help to build a more satisfying relationship. Behavioral changes should be determined independently by each person rather than each feeling "forced" by another.

> **Timing**—Discuss the problem as close as possible to the conflict's occurrence so the other person will know exactly what is being discussed. Bringing up previous situations can be viewed as holding onto "old hurts" and maintaining them simply to strike back rather than to resolve problems. Then again, there may be times when a "cooling off" period is necessary because the feelings are too intense for reasonable discussion.

Ten Tips for Maintaining Emotional Fitness

Once you become more emotionally fit, it is important to maintain what you have accomplished. The following 10 tips will help you review the ingredients of emotional health and keep you from falling back into old, detrimental habits.

1. **Become aware of your needs.** The first step is to accept yourself. Remember, the unconscious part of your brain really knows you. When you force yourself to act differently, it will show. If your life is unduly boring— or if you feel put upon or neglected—admit it and do something about it, rather than just saying, "This is the pits."

2. **Let your needs be known.** Assert yourself and clearly present your feelings without attacking others. This will prevent negative feelings from building up and getting expressed in a negative way either internally (stress) or externally (inappropriate behavior).

3. **Demonstrate behavior that reflects high self-esteem.** This can be accomplished through body language and attitude. If you look alert and interested and wear a cheerful smile, others will recognize the good feelings you have about yourself.

4. **Work to improve yourself by:**

   ➤ Learning—reading, taking classes, or working with others

   ➤ Challenges—doing something new that seems interesting and fun

   ➤ Physical health and appearance—improving nutrition, getting adequate rest and regular exercise

   ➤ Spirit—spending time with optimistic people, following a spiritual program, projecting a positive attitude

5. **Stop negative value judgments about yourself and others.** Become aware of how much energy goes into judging others vs. finding unique strengths in others to admire and relate to.

6. **Allow and plan for successes.** Emphasize what you do well. Build on the strengths you have and value. Remember that all successful people have regular failures but they do not allow themselves to be defeated by them.

7. **Think positively.** Think about your good qualities. Give yourself credit. Keep a "What I Like About Myself" journal.

8. **Learn to escape when appropriate.** It is good to meet problems head-on, but occasional sidestepping may be desirable. People often set unrealistically high standards and become frustrated when they do not achieve them. Learn to add variety to your life by planning interesting activities. Do not wait for someone else to make your life interesting.

9. **Find ways to help others.** Refocus your attention on the needs of others. Identify ways you can give to others (such as volunteering for a community project, getting involved in a church program, finding a person in need of companionship). Above all, show interest in others during normal conversation. Isolating yourself makes it difficult to enjoy good emotional health.

10. **Be willing to seek help when required.** When you have problems, find people with whom you can share them. If problems seem overwhelming, seek professional help. Professional help is indicated particularly if the intensity of the feelings does not go away after sharing them with friends or family, or if feelings of worthlessness or low self-esteem persist.

CASE STUDY: Carol Looks Ahead

Carol has been effective in dealing with the stress in her life. She has worked hard to understand herself and the way she relates to others. She has been honest about both her strengths and her weaknesses. When required, she has not been reluctant to seek help from her friends. On one occasion, she sought professional help when she encountered a particularly difficult situation.

Carol is busy in her roles as mother, wife, and employee. Despite the demands of home and career, however, she does not want to get locked into a mechanical or rigid approach to life. She feels the need for a way to manage her time effectively and to avoid becoming overwhelmed with the demands placed on her. She feels the need for emotional support from others to cope with her busy schedule. In short, Carol is open to growth and change and feels the need for an action plan to maintain the gains she has made so far.

What ideas do you have for how Carol could develop a support system to help her in the years ahead?

_____

_____

_____

_____

_____

_____

Compare your responses to the authors' suggestions in the Appendix.

Setting Personal Goals

Goals are significant because they provide direction for our lives. Life is more meaningful when we take responsibility for where we are going. Once people establish goals, they tend to meet them.

Yet few people establish long-range goals. A study at a major university showed that 20 years after graduation, only 3% of students had established clear life goals, 10% had done some work in goal setting, and an amazing 87% had never seriously worked to establish long-term personal goals.

Instead, the majority of people spend their time "meandering" through life rather than focusing on those things they really want to achieve. Thoughtful goal setting, on the other hand, can help you determine and then work on those things that are important as opposed to those that are simply fun or time fillers.

Criteria for Effective Goals

Your goals should relate to your personal life, professional life, family life, and community. And they should relate to both the long term (life goals) and the immediate future (next week).When setting personal goals, make sure they are yours—and not those that others choose for you.

A. **Criteria for personal goals can be outlined as follows:**

Are they *conceivable*? (Can I visualize them being achieved?)

Are they *believable*? (Do they make sense or are they "off the wall"?)

Are they *achievable*? (Is it realistic to assume that I can accomplish this goal?)

Are they *measurable*? (Would I know if I accomplish the goal?)

B. **Goals are not appropriate when they are:**

➤ Harmful to others

➤ Injurious to self

➤ Owned or dictated by others

C. **To be meaningful, goals should reach into areas where your potential may not be fully realized—areas beyond ordinary achievement.**

The exercise on the following pages will get you started in setting personal goals. These should be reviewed and revised regularly. It is a good idea to use a pencil for this exercise.

PERSONAL GOAL SETTING

On the lines provided, write your short-term and long-term goals in each of the five main categories of your life. There is also space at the end where you may write other goals that do not fit into the main categories.

Family Goals

Next week/month:

_____

_____

_____

Next year:

_____

_____

_____

In five years:

_____

_____

_____

Career Goals:

Next week/month:

_____

_____

_____

Next year:

_____

_____

_____

CONTINUED

In five years:

_____

_____

_____

Physical Health Goals:

Next week/month:

_____

_____

_____

Next year:

_____

_____

_____

In five years:

_____

_____

_____

Relationship Goals:

Next week/month:

_____

_____

_____

Next year:

_____

_____

_____

In five years:

_____

_____

_____

Community and Civic Goals:

Next week/month:

_____

_____

_____

Next year:

_____

_____

_____

In five years:

_____

_____

_____

Other Goals:

Next week/month:

_____

_____

_____

Next year:

_____

_____

_____

In five years:

_____

_____

_____

Reviewing Your Personal Goals

When you have finished setting your personal goals, make a copy of the pages and file them away in a safe place. Then on a special day (your birthday, New Year's Day, or a special anniversary), remove the pages from your file, find a quiet place, and review what you wrote.

A day or two later, reread this book and revise your personal goals in light of your current situation. Compare your new goals with those you previously wrote and note positive changes and areas where improvement is still needed, or desired.

If you make a habit of regularly reviewing your goals, such as once a year, you will be in a better position to keep your life directed toward the accomplishments you want to achieve. This will help you maintain good emotional health because you will have a written record of your achievements and aspirations.[*]

---

[*] For more information on setting and achieving personal goals, read *Achieving Results* by Lorna Riley, Thomson Learning/Course Technology, ©2001.

A P P E N D I X

Summary

Managing stress requires considerable determination. Let's review the main points to remember as you work to improve and maintain your emotional health:

> Understand that stress and stressful situations are all around us. Each individual has an optimum stress level that acts as motivation to accomplish goals. Unrelieved stress, however, produces physical and emotional effects that can be difficult to remedy.

> Learn your individual optimum stress level. Have both physical and emotional outlets for stress, including a regular exercise program, a support group of friends and/or co-workers, and adequate rest and nutrition.

> Aspire to develop internal awareness, acceptance, and a balanced disposition. Practice meditation to strengthen your resilience to stress.

> Work to understand yourself and others. Find ways to make personal contacts meaningful and productive, rather than negative and destructive. Value your uniqueness and build on your strengths and successes.

> Recognize, understand, and express your emotions. Work to improve yourself by learning, keeping a positive attitude, challenging yourself, and taking care of your health.

WHAT HAVE YOU LEARNED?

Life allows for many opportunities to check ourselves for improvement. This progress is often referred to as *growth*. Good emotional health is achieved through continual growth and maturation.

The assessment that follows will help you measure your progress in understanding emotional health and becoming emotionally fit. Test yourself by placing a T for true or F for false on the line following each statement.

1. Not everyone recognizes the same circumstances as stressful. _____

2. Type B personalities are people with intense drive. _____

3. Type A personalities are more successful than Type B personalities. _____

4. A denial of our feelings when we are under stress is common. _____

5. Stress can have a direct physical effect on us. _____

6. Burnout is the logical conclusion of stress over a long period of time. _____

7. We should work to eliminate all of our stress. _____

8. Balancing one's lifestyle to include play and diet control is simply a fad and not to be taken seriously. _____

9. The expression of feelings is usually a positive step toward emotional health. _____

10. Patterns of how we relate to others can be changed easily. _____

11. Conflicts should always be avoided to maintain good emotional health. _____

12. Finding somebody to be like is the best way to learn emotional health. _____

13. An emotionally healthy person should be expected to deal with all aspects of life competently. _____

CONTINUED

CONTINUED

14. The need to be appreciated is something we will outgrow. _____

15. Accepting myself may be the most important thing I can do for others to accept me. _____

16. Emotional fitness is the ability to "cope" with the joys and sorrows of life. _____

17. The ability to accept emotional support from others is a sign of emotional health. _____

18. Asserting oneself is a sign of a positive self-image. _____

19. Being "open" with another person is useful if you want to improve your relationship. _____

20. Goal setting is an important aspect in achieving emotional fitness. _____

Turn the page to check your answers.

ANSWER KEY: WHAT HAVE YOU LEARNED?

1. True

2. False

3. False

4. True

5. True

6. True

7. False

8. False

9. True

10. False

11. False

12. False

13. False

14. False

15. True

16. True

17. True

18. True

19. True

20. True

Appendix to Part 2

Comments & Suggested Responses

Maria's Overwhelming Stress

Maria needs considerable emotional support to cope with her present situation. She also must realize that she needs time for herself without feeling guilty. The burdens of motherhood can become so stressful that she may become susceptible to anxiety and physical illness unless she changes the pattern. The more Maria talks openly about her situation and the more stress "safety valves" she discovers, the better.

Appendix to Part 4

Comments & Suggested Responses

John Relates to Family and Friends

John's problems are long-standing and we cannot assume that his basic way of relating to others will change easily. The fact that John wants help in dealing with his interpersonal problems is promising. Going to his boss, wife, and friends to seek feedback about his behavior pattern is a first step. Seeking outside professional help may also be useful in helping him understand underlying causes of his combative way of relating.

Appendix to Part 5

Comments & Suggested Responses

Roger Deals with a Common Problem

Roger's withdrawal is an indication of his inability to cope with the pressures he feels. Because his behavior has changed, it is also a cause for concern. By not talking to anyone about his feelings, he adds to his potential for more severe stress. Helping Roger talk openly about his worries and fears of the future is vital.

Carol Looks Ahead

Having a life plan does not necessarily mean that spontaneity is lost. Instead, a plan makes it possible to direct and influence your future rather than simply to react to events in your life. Seeking support systems through social involvement, civic activities, or individual or group counseling can put Carol in touch with others who are succeeding in their own search. Knowing there will be ups and downs is important to avoiding becoming discouraged.

Additional Reading

Chapman, Elwood N. and Wil McKnight. *Attitude: Your Most Priceless Possession*. Boston, MA: Thomson Learning, 2002.

Chapman, Elwood N. and Barb Wingfield. *Winning at Human Relations*. Boston, MA: Thomson Learning, 2003.

Kabat-Zinn, Jon. *Full Catastrophe Living*. NY, NY: Dell Publishing Group, 1990.

Kindler, Herbert S. *Managing Disagreement Constructively*. Boston, MA: Thomson Learning, 1996.

Kravitz, S. Michael and Susan D. Schubert. *Emotional Intelligence Works*. Boston, MA: Thomson Learning, 2000.

Lloyd, Sam R. and Tina Berthelot. *Achieving Life Balance*. Boston, MA: Thomson Learning, 2005.

Myss, Caroline. *Anatomy of the Spirit*. NY, NY: Harmony Books, 1996.

Palladino, Connie. *Developing Self-Esteem*. Boston, MA: Thomson Learning, 1994.

Potter, Beverly A. *Preventing Job Burnout*. Boston, MA: Thomson Learning, 1996.

Rouillard, Larrie A. *Goals and Goal Setting*. Boston, MA: Thomson Learning, 2003.

Scott, Dru. *Stress That Motivates*. Boston, MA: Thomson Learning, 2002.

NOTES

NOTES

NOTES

NOTES

NOTES

Now Available From

THOMSON

™

NETg

Books • Videos • CD-ROMs • Computer-Based Training Products

If you enjoyed this book, we have great news for you. There are more than 200 books available in the *Crisp Fifty-Minute™ Series*. For more information contact

NETg
25 Thomson Place
Boston, MA 02210
1-800-442-7477
www.courseilt.com

Subject Areas Include:

Management
Human Resources
Communication Skills
Personal Development
Sales/Marketing
Finance
Coaching and Mentoring
Customer Service/Quality
Small Business and Entrepreneurship
Training
Life Planning
Writing